School

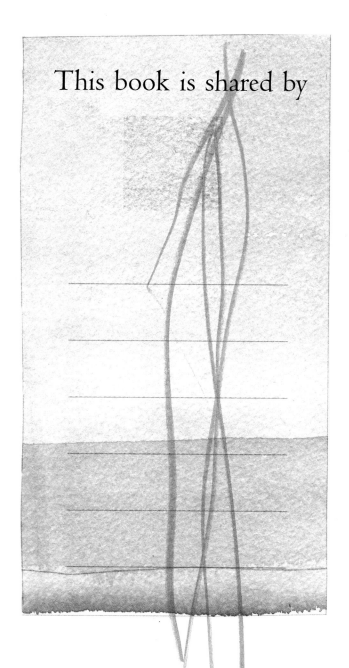

This book is shared by

For Nani, who told the best stories - N.A.
*To Avik, Sharda, Venetia, Rohan, Sahil,
Athsham & Sunara* - E.A.

This edition published 2002

First published 1999 by Mantra Publishing Ltd
5 Alexandra Grove, London N12 8NU

Printed in Italy

سميرة في الْعيد
Samira's Eid

Nasreen Aktar

Illustrated by Enebor Attard

Arabic translation by Azza Habashi

Mantra

كان الْوقت رمضان وَكان الكل صائم ، ولكن الأَطفال كانوا مشغولين
بعمل بطاقات التهنئة بالْعيد .
"هذه للجدة في المستشفى" قالت سميرة وهي تغلق الْظرف .
سأل حسن : "هل ستتحسن حالتها؟"
"نعم ، ولكن الْعيد سوف لا يكون سعيدا بدونها . "

It was during Ramadan, when everybody was fasting, that the children
were busy making cards.
"This one's for Nani in hospital," said Samira, closing the envelope.
"Will she get better?" asked Hassan.
"Yes, but Eid won't be the same without her."

ودخلت الأمّ في الْحال وقالت : "تذكرا أنتما صائمان غدا . "
"هل سيكون متعبا؟" سأل حسن . فأجابت الأمّ :
"لا بل ستشعر بالتعب . ولذا اذهب ونم بسرعة الآن . "

Just then, Mum walked in. "Remember you're fasting tomorrow," she said.
"Will it hurt?" asked Hassan.
"No, but you will feel tired. So go to sleep quickly now," answered Mum.

في الْصباح التالي وقبل شروق الْشمس تناولت سميرة وحسن سحورهما .
"تناولا كل طعامكما ، فإنه وقت طويل حتي طعام الْعشاء" ذكرتهما الأَم .

The next morning before sunrise, Samira and Hassan had their breakfast.
"Eat up! It's a long time till dinner," Mum reminded them.

وعندما جاء وقت الْغداء لم يستطع حسن أن يمنع نفسه من الْشكوي،
"أنا جدّ جوعان. أنا اريد سمبوسا."
"وأنا جوعانة أيضا، ولكن فكّر في كل الْناس الْصائمين مثلنا،"
قالت سميرة.

But by lunch time, Hassan couldn't stop himself
complaining, "I'm sooo hungry. I want a samosa."
"I'm hungry too, but think of all the people who are
fasting just like us," said Samira.

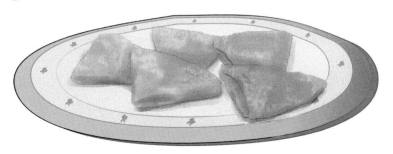

"وفكّر كذلك في هؤلاء النّاس الذين لا يأكلون سوي وجبة واحدة باليوم، " قالت الأمّ واضعة ذراعها حول حسن.

"أنا لا أحب ذلك، " قال حسن.

"حسنا وهم كذلك لا يحبون ذلك، " قالت سميرة. "لذلك ندفع الزّكاة. "

"And think of all the people who can only have one meal a day," said Mum, putting her arm around Hassan.

"I wouldn't like that," said Hassan.

"Well, they don't like it either," said Samira. "That's why we give zakat."

وأخيرا جاء وقت الْعشاء، وكانت الأُمَّ قد أعدت أطعمتهما المفضلة .
قالت سميرة لوالدها : "لقد استطعنا أن نصوم مثلكم . "
تبسم الأَب وقال : "كنت متأكدا من استطاعتكما . كيف تشعرون الآن؟"
تأوه الأَطفال وقالوا : "جوعانين . "

At last it was time for dinner and Mum had prepared their favourite food.
"Dad, we did it! We fasted just like you," said Samira.
"I knew you could do it," said Dad, smiling. "How do you feel?"
"Hungry," they groaned.

وفي ليلة الْعيد أعلن في الإذاعة رؤية الهلال .
وجرت سميرة بسرعة إلي غرفة حسن لتزف إليه الْخبر .

The night before Eid, the radio announced
the sighting of the new moon. Quickly Samira
ran to Hassan's room to tell him the news.

وقالت : "لقد ظهر الهلال . "

"أين؟" سأل حسن واسرع إلي الْنافذة .

"في مكة طبعا وليس هنا ! "

"The new moon has just been seen," she said.
"Where?" asked Hassan, dashing to the window.
"In Mecca of course, not here!"

Very early, while everyone was still asleep, Samira and Hassan gazed
 at the new moon, so thin and pale in the morning sky.
"Look Hassan, there it is," whispered Samira.
"Eid Mubarak, Samira," said Hassan.

مبكرا جدا، بينما كل الْناس نائمون، سميرة وحسن حملقا في
الهلال الْجديد، نحيف جدا وباهت في سماء الْصبح.
"انظر يا حسن، ها هو ذا" همست سميرة.
"عيد مبارك، يا سميرة" قال حسن.

رجعت سميرة إلي غرفتها فوجدت ملابسها الْجديدة علي سريرها .
وبرفق رفعت الْقميص الذي صنعته لها أمها إلي أعلا .
وعندئذ أيقنت أنّه الْعيد .

Back in her room, Samira saw her new clothes lying on the bed.
Gently she lifted the shalwar-kameez that her mum had made and
held it up. It really is Eid, she thought.

وعندما تجهز كل واحد توجهت الأسرة إلي المسجد مرددين
"عيد مبارك" لكل أصدقائهم في الطّريق .
وداخل المسجد استمعوا للإمام وأدوا الصّلاة .

When everyone was ready, the family left for the mosque.
"Eid Mubarak," they called out to their friends on the way.
Inside the mosque they prayed and listened to the Imam.

وفي خارج المسجد كانت جموع من الْناس يبتسمون
ويحتضن بعضهم الْبعض . فجأة رأت سميرة معلمتها
وصاحت، "انظر ياحسن الْسيدة قدير مقبلة علينا . "

Outside there were lots of people smiling and
hugging each other. Suddenly, Samira saw her teacher.
"Look Hassan, it's Mrs Qadir coming over here."

"عيد مبارك يا سميرة، عيد مبارك يا حسن" قالت الْسيدة قدير
ووضعت في يد كل منهماهدية .
فشكراها وسألاها "كيف عرفت أننا هنا؟"
فتبسمت المعلمة وقالت "المعلمون يعرفون مثل هذه الأشياء . "

"Eid Mubarak, Samira and Hassan," said Mrs Qadir, placing a small
present in their hands.
"Thank you," they said. "But how did you know that we'd be here?"
"Teachers know these things," replied Mrs Qadir, smiling.

عندما رجعوا إلي الْبيت وجدوا كومة من الكروت منتظرة أن تفتح .
"هذه واحدة من الْخالة ياسمين، فهذه من الْعم اقبال" قالت سميرة .
"ولكن أين كارت الْجدة؟"

When they arrived home, they found a pile of Eid cards waiting to be opened. "Here's one from Aunty Yasmin, and this one's from Uncle Iqbal," said Samira. "But where *is* Nani's card?"

أجابت الأُمُّ : "ربما ستأتي في الدورة الثّانية للبريد . الآن اسرعا
وساعداني في إعداد المائدة . "
"انظر إليَّ كل ذلك الطّعام" تعجبت سميرة وقالت "يا له من عيد !"

"Maybe it will come in the second post. Now hurry up and help me
get these dishes onto the table," said Mum.
"Look at all that food," gasped Samira. "What a feast!"

دق جرس الْباب مرات ومرات بينما الْخالات والْعمات والْأعمام
والْجيران يصلون . وكان هناك كثير من الْقبلات والْأحضان
والْضحكات والْهدايا . لم تكن سميرة وحسن يصدقا أعينهما .
وأعلن الْوالد : "تفضلوا اجلسوا، الْطعام جاهز ."

The door bell rang, again and again, as aunts and uncles, friends and
neighbours arrived. There was hugging and kissing, laughter and presents.
Samira and Hassan could hardly believe their eyes.
"Come and sit down everyone. The food is ready," announced Dad.

قال الْوالد : "اجلسي هنا يا سميرة . "
وقالت سميرة : "ولكن هذا المكان خاليا . "
"لم يعد خاليا" أجاب صوت معروف .

"Samira, come and sit here," said Dad.
"But this chair's empty," said Samira, pointing to the chair next to her.
"Not for long," said a familiar voice.

"عيد مبارك لكل واحد" قالت الْجدة وهي تبتسم. "لم أثق في هذه المستشفي أن تحضر الكارت في الْوقت المناسب، فلم يكن أمامي إلّا أن أحضرها بنفسي."

صحكت سميرة وسألت: "ولكن كيف حضرت إلي هنا؟"

"Eid Mubarak everyone," said Nani, smiling. "Samira, I just couldn't trust that hospital to get the card to you on time. So what could I do but bring it myself?" Samira laughed. "But how did you get here?"

"تلك قصة طويلة، ولكن أولا هذا شيء صغير لك ولحسن"
أجابت الْجدة .
وعندما فتحت سميرة وحسن الهدية وجدا بداخلها كتاب .
ولكن هذا ليس كتابا عاديا، وتسببت الإبتسامة علي وجوههما في
ضحك كل الموجودين .

"That is a long story, but first, a little something for you and Hassan," said Nani.
When Samira and Hassan opened their present, they found a book inside. But
this was no ordinary book, and the smiles on their faces made everybody laugh.

وفي آخر النّهار تكوّرت سميرة في حضن الْجدة علي
الكنبة وطلب حسن من الْجدة: "احكي لنا الْقصة يا جدتي."
"الْوقت رمضان وكان الكل صائم، ولكن الأطفال. . ."

By the end of the day, a happy Samira had curled up on the sofa next to Nani.
"Nani, tell us your story now," asked Hassan.
"Well, it was during Ramadan, when everybody was fasting, that the children were..